D1558230

OMNIVM LVX CIVIVM

BOSTON
PUBLIC
LIBRARY

DEAR
BLOOD

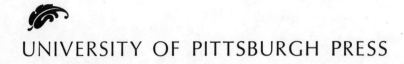
UNIVERSITY OF PITTSBURGH PRESS

Dear Blood

LEONARD NATHAN

Published by the University of Pittsburgh Press, Pittsburgh, Pa. 15260
Copyright © 1980, by Leonard Nathan
All rights reserved
Feffer and Simons, Inc., London
Manufactured in the United States of America

Library of Congress Cataloging in Publication Data

Nathan, Leonard, 1924–
  Dear blood.

  (Pitt poetry series)
  I. Title.
PS3564.A849D4   811'.5'4   79-13113
ISBN 0-8229-3407-8
ISBN 0-8229-5312-9 pbk.

Some of the poems in this book appeared (occasionally in a slightly different form) in *Abraxas, Beloit Poetry Journal, Berkeley Poetry Review, Bits, Choice, Chowder Review, Coup and Other Poems, Epoch, Iowa Review, Marilyn, New Salt Creek Reader, Poetry Now, The Sole Proprietor, Sunstone Review, Twelve Poems,* and *Via.* They are reprinted by permission of the editors. "Gap," © 1975 and "Widowhood," © 1976 by The New Yorker Magazine, Inc. "At the Border," "Evolution," "Hole," "Poem for an Occasion," and "The Apple Tree" were originally published in *The Ohio Review.* "Reflection," "Selling," and "Simples" first appeared in *San Jose Studies.* "The Lover," © 1977 by Washington and Lee University, is reprinted from *Shenandoah:* The Washington and Lee University Review with the permission of the editor. "Entrance," "Confession," and "Makings" (originally titled "The Kit") first appeared in *Three Rivers Poetry Journal,* copyright © 1977, 1979 by Three Rivers Press.

Thanks are due to the University of California and the Guggenheim Foundation for providing time and funds that helped the author complete this book.

*The publication of this book is supported by grants
from the National Endowment for the Arts
in Washington, D.C., a Federal agency,
and the Pennsylvania Council on the Arts.*

CONTENTS

CONTENTS

CONTENTS

III. WOUNDED SYSTEMS

CONTENTS

I

Yours Truly

CONFESSION

This is meant to warn you
but cannot, nor me either.

I heard it from the foghorn
crying all night on the Bay.

Terrible powers are bearing down
and do not even want to.

I caught it in the chill wind
off the mountain north.

Old men wait in the cold
and do not know they wait for nothing.

Your own dear blood whistled it up
unthinking through frayed vents.

And it was in the meek gasp
between one lost life and another.

Think of the endless mouthings of fish
or a flute blown over by leaves.

All I can do is take your breath
for a little music.

WAITING

In some worlds
there's no word
for loneliness
because people are everywhere,
even in stones and stars.

I dreamed grandfather,
dead, sat waiting for me
in a small room
with no window,
his hands folded on his cane.

God also must be alone
with Himself waiting
in a solitude that contains
us all, but so pure
only the dead can feel it.

In His dream
each stone has only to wait
and each star, and I also,
for the children to enter.
And it's no place for tears.

GAP

This is the gap
for one butterfly to pass through,
a lucky break in the senseless green.

It's there by the grace of God,
who is I think the absence of a spider
at this particular time and place.

You may think He's the absence only
of leaves now dead or, more incredible yet,
the presence of the one butterfly.

HABAKKUK

In conversations with the Lord
you can't tell always
who's talking to whom.

Maybe it's the wind
on high places or the vision down
on all the nasty creepings below.

Mountains, rivers, whole oceans
shrivel under your stare and the light
rings in your temples.

Bone rot and shook foundations,
hands sprouting horns, stones crying in walls—
you're going crazy.

Who wouldn't, seeing what we can see?
Lord, we'll tell them what they are.
Lord, are You listening?

ENTRANCE

This is where you came in,
this shadowed cleft.

It's no vent
for expanding good nature
or breach for the evolution
of God
though it was brought roses once
and sung to.

But all the suasions of spring
are lost to it now.

It listens instead
to something far back,
listens as an old dog would
or stony ruin, with the dignity
of things reduced
to their least selves.

WIDOWHOOD

It's as if the wife
of King Lear wandered onstage
after the play
and since there was no script
they had to hustle up
a few lines of pious resignation
to staunch the tears—
the cue for a heads-up exit,
while in the unlit alley outside,
its right rear door flung open,
the black Buick from the nursing home
snarled under the toe of a booted lackey.

OPPORTUNITY

We thought we owned the apple
having raised it simply
to bite at our pleasure.

But this worm
found it a sweet way
into its own ripeness.

That was a mouthful
of sour knowledge
for spitting out.

Could there be a higher purpose
that used us both
toward its own ripening?

Ha, say the dark seeds,
ha, and exult
to the core.

SWARM

Have you missed something
lately—

Say, a great purpose
humming in full accord
to its necessary end?

Or a wild stinging sweetness
pulsing like a struck gong
of obscure gold?

Or God's blind eye
pullulating
out of the blue?

Well here it is
hung from a branch
the moment before history begins
and the homely labors of the hive.

THE SHADOW

Out of the blind genes
of its darkness
it hunted everywhere
for Substance.

Its dreams were only
of Substance,
clear as an angel
seated under a plane tree
somewhere eastward
waiting.

It tamed wolves,
taught itself prayers,
built traps called towns,
fought other competing shadows,
constructed flight—
all to hunt Substance,
and every next day
rose again
to kiss the wife
and go out—
the wife who stood solidly there
hating Substance.

THE INHERITANCE

You think you knew
your father?

Feeding pigeons
from a soft hat
he said
all I wanted for them
was sun and a little green,
someplace to be lonely in without shame.

My father
didn't even wear a hat.

DUSTING

The universe under the light
is a still suspension
of many gray particles
glinting faintly as they sink
according to the law.

Some say there's life out there
if only we find the right signal.
What do you think they'd understand—
a little flare for loneliness
or, maybe, a far cry against the law?

EVOLUTION

You've seen how it works —
backwards in huge silence.

So the cat's got your tongue but can't talk,
the butterfly your vagrant grace
without a reason, while your muffled heart
races the fox to its last hole.

And we who began as human, modeling
love for certain Italian Masters,
now slide by, low in shadow,
or freeze, hoping to be taken for stone.

YOURS TRULY

Sometimes a wild thing
will walk right out of the woods
into your hands
and you, thinking of something else,
kneel and receive it
as if it were yours to stroke
from the very first
and then it's gone,
the after-color of fox fading
into the woods and the woods
darkening shut behind it
while you stare down at spread hands
measuring an emptiness
nothing else can fill

and this is love
and this is a judgment.

THE FLOOR JOB

When I pulled these lines up
stave by stave
I found in the dank below
a clutch of snakes churning.

Yellow rings
on beaded orange and black bands,
beautiful
and maybe poisonous.

I could have
broken their backs,
studied
or tamed them.

But laid back down
stave by stave
these lines
replacing only the bad ones,
which was my job.

THE WATCH

You'll forgive me maybe
if I admit that while you were busy
doing what was necessary
I took the time to watch
a blue light in the harbor
flashing softly once every three seconds.

Nothing much happened.
The vast solitude of a tanker
veered by in fog
shyly averting the one shock
that might have run us greatly together
and all was well, all was well.

CREED

Listening for reality,
I hear instead strange sounds—
far-off barking, wind or tide
sifting through pines, a soft spell
of mere breathing.

           My faith
without the least effort
has been in those things
from the very start
as my foot every step
of the way has believed in the ground.

II

Devotions

HOLE

The mouse crawled through it,
the snake after him
and you're next.

Did you think
because Socrates went through
and Saint Francis
it was going to be bigger?

They also squeezed every hope
into its least possibility,
shedding layer after layer
to slide, tongue flicking,
into the rank darkness.

O yes,
the self is that small.

FAMILY CIRCLE

When I left Ithaca
for the great action
I was clean-cut, smartly
purposeful and nice
by inexperience.

I thought I'd be back soon
because the earth is flatly
a circle, but found,
though you want to go straight,
what survives is bent.

Well, here I am finally,
beat-up pilgrim to a homely shrine,
my bare rock and old woman
willing glumly to receive what I offer—
a scar and a tall story.

I see my son's eyes lift slyly
from his plate, asking what it was for—
struggle, shipwreck, and such lies.
It was for this, sonny, this:
my eating and your asking.

POEM FOR AN OCCASION

If you said
exactly
what the occasion required
(snow on the ground
dirty and the sky bellying down
like weathered canvas),
enough anyway
to cover the facts
(she at the window
looking out on another stretch of boredom
only vaster),
you would have satisfied
a minimal requirement
(like the lowest-priced coffin
for someone once loved
beyond words).

THE LOVER

Out of the old trunk
he took a flute,
a lantern,
a fountain,
the moon,
summer,
Italy,
the death mask of Byron.

And as he went down to play
a suite of moths followed him.

In the dark we thought
they were his wings.

THE HEARING

Which one is crying
outside?

You say
it's she whose bones
were found in the creek bed
last August
sacrificed,
or she whose small wings
spread fire as they flared
toward us
from the distant bombing,
or she who rode off
with other children
on a crusade through flowers
never seen again.

I say it may be simply
the wind's younger sister
which is enough
to level this house
to the foundations
leaving only guilt standing

like a cold chimney.

MEMO

Who wrote
"I love you daddy"
on this white page?

The littlest daughter did
on this white page
under which lie concealed
thirty virginal pages
for later messages.

TENDRIL

Born for this world
you'll be tough as rope
five years from now
when we'll remember
the first maiden curl
reaching
delicately
out
for a blind feel,
and pity ourselves
gripped,
gripping,
to the death.

VIGILS

The blind face
of the house
expects all day someone
who isn't coming
through this rain
or ever,
though the windows go on
staring into the dark.

Your mother's wet glasses
glittered so in the lamp
when there was no one left
to sew for.

DEVOTIONS

(after Rimbaud)

To Sister Mary Louise
still waiting for us in the room
with one iron chair and the parakeet of her forgiveness.

To Sister Marta
who by chance saw the killing
over the shoulder of her partner
and so keeps dancing, dancing.

To Sister Jade who was done to
so fast she never had time to cry out.

To her younger sister
ditto.

To the doers
now caught in iron and chanting
through gray slats that Sister
Mary Louise has forgotten them.

To tide pools
when the tide is out.

To infinite repetitions
of patience for no reason more than the sea's
for rising and falling.

And so again to Sister Mary Louise
her iron hair crowning a mind
full of betrayals,
her chest rising and falling
in the violet dusk.

REFLECTION

(after Stramm)

He'd break her
because he's stone
and she's glass.

If time hadn't stopped cold
at 3:20 P.M.
two years back on the stairs
she'd be a handful of red slivers.

But he's locked still
loving in his hardness
as she flashes faithfully
from far off.

THE SHRINE

I've waited for you
in this room, day by day
excluding what wasn't needed
until there's only this green cushion
tassled at the corners
and, in the far wall, a recess
for an orange vase with three white irises,
and a scroll stroked with ink
meant to be a bird flying
or how it feels to fly.

I've made good talk for us both
over tea while snow quietly aged
the pines outside and settled like ash
on the pond where carp
deepen the shadow.

Were you the one
who passed on the way
to some consummation,
whose smile I mistook
and so built all this
and so must live
in the wrong hope?

SUICIDE

Sometimes
you find a fallen sparrow
with no note
pinned to its dusty wing
and the wing oddly twisted
but there's no time
for persuasion or the ambulance,
no time but now
stiffening in your right hand
which also holds
the infinite stillness
of the other world
and fits so snugly
you stare hard
for some reason
but read there only
the future in it.

AT THE BORDER

They shake hands,
passing fear
back and forth
through the hard skin of habit,
then the father
turning
fades to the color
of a mole's coat
or river under rain
while the son
feels his hand
already forgetting
everything
but the pressure.

THE GARDEN

This garden is not for you
Greensleeves
or Rose Red either.

It's for her,
the hanged daughter of poverty.

It's down there in the essentials
of hairy chickweed,
of glass shard and the chill
of brown-water ruts in March.

It's for her to remember in
(if she wants)
back to her seventh birthday
before she knew every bad thing.

It's for her to persist in
(if she still cares)
with the shy subversive
faith of grass.

IN SANTIAGO DE CHUCO

Black hat for conscience
black suit for defiance
black shoes for going to
or coming from a funeral
limping silent and steady
without a mother or money
his purpose narrow as a sword
glittering and dusty
under the afternoon sun
no wine guitars or roses
only one dog barking
along the sharp edge
of his path so pointed
he becomes at its far end
before dissolving in light
a furious black period.

ADVENT

It's the lull in traffic after dusk
when lamps shine up meekly
all down the long slope that huddles
dark in darker waters.

There's nothing like it in the world
and it is the world simple and strange as oxen
waiting to be led in from the cold field
if someone only knew how.

GIFT

The last timber wolf
died before I knew it
north in snow-haggered pines
while I was hunting a gift
for your birthday.

In the solitude of failure
no wrong choice is forgiven
and what I hold out
is only local love remembering
one of a kind.

III

Wounded Systems

VISION FOR THE TIME

This is not what the Lord said
and needs no saying
maybe only a witness
maybe no witness, only
a runner running through it
and away into the country
out of the state, the nation,
out of the usual sleep and smash
into the solitude of one decent idea

therefore make it simple I thought
and swift so that he who runs
can read it
        read it and run.

THE ELECTION

How did the stones vote
this time?

They voted for hardness
and few words

as the trees voted
for slow growth
upward and a shedding
of dead dependents.

And the men?

They voted against
themselves again
and for fire
which they thought they
could control,
fire
which voted for blackened stumps
and no more elections.

CANDIDATE

Left or right
he didn't know which way
to turn, which profile
was more winning.

Facing us fully
he's vulnerable
as an honest man
caught in a lie.

AT THE WELL

Does this water
taste of oil to you?

They say drink
what you don't use in the car.

Do these pipes
serving the wrong thirst
reach down to the wrong assumption
so pumping a septic mix
into the pitcher?

They say it's all a waste
anyhow
so accept it.

Do you feel bad
swallowing that?

They say this numbness
is life adapting to new conditions.

The numb parts of me
believe them.

COUP

That chair
isn't yours anymore.

Noon
when bells shed iron
on the dusty sleep of the poor
we took your chair.

The Republic
is now a wall
for you to die against
and (after a whitewash)
a background
for our smiles.

No hard feelings.

DISCOVERY

We found the truth
but you didn't like it
and so left us.

You didn't like it
because it explained everything
and made jokes on the side.

You said it wasn't that easy,
that amusing, that much better
than the old error.

So you went back out
to experience, writing how strange
it was, how great.

We made a joke about that too,
then took the truth out of its box
and asked it to make you sorry.

SELLING

My persuasion
is a shoe size,
bifocals, a dislike
for persimmons and foreigners.

I know just
where the shoe pinches,
the eye blurs,
the stomach turns.

I can adjust up,
I can adjust down,
I can be the spitting image.
Believe me.

LAW AND ORDER

After the old gangster said
of a young revolutionary:
I could eat that bastard's
two eyeballs like cherries,
he added:
when I killed people
they asked for it.

No offense.

GAME

When I was eagle
you shot me
out of the sky.

When I was egret
you stood up in the reeds
and blew out my right eye.

When I'm human
you'll give me
a reason.

ARTICLE OF FAITH

Where they fell
the grass is now greener
and no one is left to know
but their god.
Protect us, they cried,
but He couldn't.
Be with us anyhow, they said
and the grass is now greener.

TO BE READ TO YOURSELF
IN A PUBLIC PLACE, JULY 4, 1976

1

If you start in loneliness
and buckskin.

If you cross rivers with no visible farther bank,
decades of hot grass,
cold uncut altitudes.

If you kill buffaloes
and braves for plausible reasons.

If you look out at the Pacific
and feel unsatisfied.

If you find gold—just like that—
under your feet.

What are you supposed
to do now?

Is America space merely to be crossed
over and over by loneliness
whose far edge, however lucky, is dissatisfaction?

Through iced hemlocks and snow a buck
still listens as though death were just hunting
enough to get through winter like a Cayuga.

As before we came,
as if we never arrived.

2

Gulls poise delicately
over the mincing waters,
chopped jade fending off
the sunset with a green
windy radiance.

Everyone in the bar
stares out the great window
at this honest wonder,
their lonely drinks
hanging in midair.

The gulls alone are not taken in.
At the first symptom
of garbage
they shriek and plunge.

3

Through the thin hill fog
the young city across the Bay
is an amber nebula.

All possibilities await you there,
every disappointment
and your heart goes out.

Especially it goes out,
racing over the windy bridge,
to disappointment.

4

On the sink of the Golden Motel washroom
the water glass is swathed
in fresh sterile paper.

The Old World
doesn't care if a wall needs paint
or smells of piss.

Here it seems I've got to believe
no one ever lived (or died)
in this room.

And when I leave
it will be made to look
as if I'd never been.

5

Is it the Game
or the Talk Show tonight?

Is it the Murder
or Old Comedy?

It's not the News.
Who would believe it?

6

It's a brand new morning
to rise, shower,
put on clean underwear,
start over again,
routinely reborn
as if Voltaire had never lived,
or Bismarck or Tolstoy.

53

What do you do
with this well-meaning idiot,
the American?

Nod and cheer him on.

Did you expect what began in hope
not to develop its habit
any more than a gray branch
gives up trying to thrust
its blind little horns into spring?

Nod and cheer me on.

7

Five motorcycles stand
outside a small tavern,
giving off a dark heat
in the oily dusk.

You think of hard-ridden mustangs
waiting patiently for their riders,
of greased leather and gun metal,
of something no law contains.

Pretending not to notice,
you drive on, but the sulking power
of it follows your vulnerable back,
like a taunt, for many blocks.

8

I write you out of fear
and out of love.

Yesterday your grandchildren discovered
in the playground a murder.

Under some kind of bush. It will change
their lives, how we can't tell.

They were playing after rain. You know—
clear sweet air and puddle-splash.

Police were professional, but ashamed,
wouldn't answer questions.

Last night was a new silence at dinner.
Crocuses grew on that very spot.

A sudden show of gold in spring.
It was just a young girl.

Stay well. The children ask to be remembered.
They're playing now out back.

I hear their cries.

9

There's too much to consecrate.

What the poor have done
to survive in all these exclusive riches.

What the old have done
to endure all this private newness.

What the intelligent have done
just to stay sane crossing pure mineral space.

What the small have done
not to be crushed under the shadows of redwoods.

What the good have done
to go on when all they get is a garbled echo for their trouble.

What couples have done
to love anyway after the end of credit.

What the lone brave has done
to go on dancing even while they built a shabby institution
around him.

These are huge stars they struggle under in America
and adore, the cold gorgeous star-system.

How they lose and persist anyway,
out to discover the New World.

It's this failure to be consecrated
and nevertheless persist.

To persist and to be consecrated.
Done. Done in the poor unprecedented doing.

LINCOLN

This, his last speech,
composed between theater and deathbed,
is still to be heard.

In its preamble of pain
he draws all creatures equal into the nation
of his pity

then lowers their hurt cries
gently down to the faith of his breath as it softens
into a prayer of grass

and ends praising
the wounded system that called him out
to his own doubtful election.

LETTER

Dear Antigone,
after going over all the arguments
pro and con, I'm as divided as ever,
but when the last word dies away,
I know you're right.

Everybody does,
that's why Creon has to bury you
every time the state can't make children
obey the letters of the law
that don't spell love.

And that's why I stand here watching it all,
glad no one has asked me to help,
my littlest daughter's hand in mine,
her eyes looking up with a sad trust,
already forgiving.

THE WEIGHING

Balanced Hitler
with Gandhi, Stalin
with Tolstoy, Nero
with Francis, canceling
each by the other,
leaving on this shore
only a low dune flower
to the good, a tough bit of gold
that bees fight the wind over
for a little sweetness.

Who could have dreamed
the scales would tip
in our favor?

IV
Sightings

SIGHTINGS

You've seen at dusk
how far-off traffic can catch sunlight
as it sinks to merge so many
into a single moving lustre,
and have thought of a blaze of angels—
but no, only spirits briefly fused
by the drive toward home.

Think of that drive,
a million lonely wishes made one
and lit like unearthly love
that could kindle a world,
and think also of your own relentless wish,
doubtful and visionary.

SIMPLES

God must have been simple
to have included the dandelion
with old age and gladness
in His catalogue.

Neither are there weeds
in the random garden
of small children, only
brief wonders to kneel at.

When the yellow fool in the grass
turns gray, one breath
can seed the air with messages
transparent as angels.

MAKINGS

B fitted snugly with A,
a black pine on a green slope
afterlit by a fallen sun,
and C also slipped into place,
a small cabin in the pine shadow,
but D, however hard we forced,
wouldn't be joined, the death of a child
in there—the death of a child?

So we kneel here holding D
over the darkening landscape
like the wrong star foreboding
only a small absence to shepherds
and sages who might look up
anxious for directions.

THE APPLE TREE

In this world
no fewer than forty-two species
balance off
life and death—
worm and mantis,
beetle and spider
hovered over by the wasp.

In its shade
she leans on his shoulder
like peace
on the shoulder of war,
a pledged couple.

If you had a choice
would you be happy
in this world
if you had a choice?

VAN GOGH

One lark over a green cornfield
will hold earth straining in place
and keep the windy sky lit if skittish.

But crows can suddenly set all yellow
loose from wheat, flap heaven
dark and shut the one road through a harvest.

Blame it on the crows, though the lark too
is a delusion, or on seeds
coded to serve blindly for bread alone.

Stars will sicken anyway, the sun
burst and hills slide down like water.
Blame it on water then, but paint it right.

STRAITS

Think that every time through
is the last, that never is rock
so hard, mist so thick,
self so shrunk and tender.

Think back to the cold body
of water behind, brawling
and bitter, and the one ahead,
warm, we're told, and sweet.

Or consider this a good story
only for faith in which those
who are nothing if not faithful
offer their lives as a prayer.

EYES ONLY

O lord,
yes, I've seen them,
Unidentified Flying Objects,

and been talked to out of tule fog
by gentle things from stars
suggesting peace on earth.

I've even detected in your eyes at times
something alien and tender
prompting me to do only what I should.

So I say there's a mystery
in flight yet and a strange kindness
still to be accounted for.

They study these saving wonders
like enemy secrets, but so far
find them only human.

CONSIDERATIONS

1

The apple tree works
all year toward leaflessness.
I undress every night
without thinking.

2

I dream you a horse
forbidden in the city.
When I'm cured
I'll dream you a Chevrolet.

3

A fox doubles through the old
dog's sleep. Let him be.
Think of waking up
in this world.

KIND

I hadn't noticed
till a death took me outside
and left me there
that grass lifts so quietly
to catch everything
we drop and we drop
everything.

TO TRANSCEND THE CAT

1

Out of a half-
demolished church,
its chancel the clear sky,
we saw sparrows
flock suddenly up
startled as spirits
dissolving deep
into radiant vacancy.

2

Sparrow
is your basic bird.

He can't live
by intimations.

Where he flies
there's a good reason.

When he sings
necessity keeps time.

3

One maple leaf remains
of summer—I try to let it be,
a lone survivor.

But can't. A thin stem
links it to a branch

distracted by sparrows
as I'm distracted
from onlyness as from
a last delusion.

4

Preston knows
Acer macrophyllum
as a common ornamental tree,
the Big Leaf Maple,
tolerant but preferring
moist sites for its fast rise
and shallow roots that support
the whole system
(including winged seeds)
under a compact crown.

Preston knows.

5

When branches glow
in the late sun
birds seem dark buds
of fire on a candelabrum
and the whole system
celebrates.
       Preston,
do you also celebrate?

6

Sparrow perched
on a warm bough
feels he was made
for this world
and so sings.

He's forgotten
his own strangeness.

It's his faith
to forget.

7

Fluttering at
the glass turret
of Mrs. Miller's feeder
(a column uplifted
to transcend the cat)
the hungry soul of sparrow
is reduced to pure
twittering want
the cat studies
in his enforced leisure.

8

I'm a student too.
I try to connect birds
with trees (and cats).

So far it's just theory.

9

Mr. Zane, eighty-two,
manages fifteen stairs
in twenty minutes, slower
than a sparrow's fall
to the landing below
where he stands
like an old stump
remembering.
                    It's our faith
to remember everything.

10

The chisel
that gouged rot
out of the heartwood
left a shocked mouth,
a gasp of shadow.

Now the tree speaks
for itself. Now
it stands for itself.

11

Nevertheless
every time sparrow
settles on the maple
he creates the world
singing it up
from its dark origins
to a dome of light.

Who am I
not to accept creation
whatever it is?

CLOSURE

My mother died as though,
going out a door, she closed it
softly so it wouldn't disturb
my father watching TV.

Why fuss? Why make something
out of it? But isn't the habit
of life to make something
out of everything?

She knew that, but this once
refused, maybe because she saw
in that doorway at last death
wasn't a creature of habit.

GRACE

Something
we think will save us yet
but we don't know it, or know it
but don't yet know it will save us.

We look around.
Is it you, love, dear other, offering all
we want till some defect or little death
and we're lost? It's not love.

There are certain words
said to change everything if well meant
but no one alive knows how to pronounce them
and the grass is mum. It's not words.

Of course, there's always distance,
a haze of superhuman forms, and futures
wide as the sky, but such foresights
arrive in the dark and it's not heaven.

And yet we believe,
amazed at sweet water or a sudden glance,
forgetting even hope in what is given.
We look around and are grateful.

HIEROGLYPH

I think the soul
is Egyptian
carved small on an old stone face
in a long parade of figures
some even bird-headed
all fixed and facing a far-off meaning
to be deciphered at last
by a brighter future.

Much is behind you
not to be known
and much ahead
of where you stand only for one true sound
(less maybe than a word)
before knowledge passes on.

Be ready,
be clear.

AND FINALLY

It's a plain table,
beech or alder,
the grain humbly confessing itself
through clear varnish.

The cup sitting alone
on its surface is cracked but good enough
to hold what winter requires
and a bent serviceable spoon.

One of the two chairs is for you
though both may be empty
when you arrive to find
a book lying beside the cup.

It's the very one
you always intended to read—
anywhere in it you turn
will be your story.

BOSTON PUBLIC LIBRARY

3 9999 00192 634 2

WITHDRAWN

No longer the property of the
Boston Public Library.
Sale of this material benefits the Library.

Boston Public Library

10/80

COPLEY SQUARE
GENERAL LIBRARY

PS3564
.A849D4

9800175320

The Date Due Card in the pocket indi-
cates the date on or before which this
book should be returned to the Library.

Please do not remove cards from this
pocket.